HOPE|EXPLORED

WHAT'S THE BEST FUTURE
YOU COULD EVER IMAGINE?

HANDBOOK

Hope Explored Handbook
Copyright © Christianity Explored Ministries 2022
Reprinted 2022
www.hope.explo.red

Published by:
The Good Book Company

thegoodbook.com | thegoodbook.co.uk
thegoodbook.com.au | thegoodbook.co.nz | thegoodbook.co.in

CHRISTIANITY
E**X**PLORED
MINISTRIES

ISBN: 9781784986827 | Printed in Turkey

Design by André Parker

CONTENTS

	Welcome	5
SESSION 1	Hope	7
SESSION 2	Peace	17
SESSION 3	Purpose	25
EXTRAS	Can we rely on Luke's Gospel?	33
	How to keep exploring	37

WELCOME TO
HOPE|EXPLORED

There are few emotions more powerful than hope. It's a spark inside you that brings a smile to your lips, a light that shows on your face, a feeling that lifts your head and pulls you forward. Hope is what keeps us alive.

These days hope often feels hard to come by. But real hope is what the Christian faith claims to offer: a joyful expectation for the future, based on true events in the past, which changes everything about my present.

It sounds good… but is it true? Whatever you do or don't believe, this series is your opportunity to explore, to discuss, to question, to discover. This is *Hope Explored*.

Key

▷ Watch a film

🗩 Discuss a question

📖 Explore a Bible passage

SESSION 1
HOPE

▷ WATCH: Hope Part 1

- Hope is a wonderful thing – but few things are more crushing than when our hopes are disappointed.

- A hope worth having needs to…
    - be true.
    - deliver what it promises.
    - be for something that will last.

- The Christian faith is all about hope: a joyful expectation for the future, based on true events in the past, which changes everything about my present.

DISCUSS

How much hope we have will depend on where we've been, where we are, and where we think we're going. Some of us may be searching for hope; others of us may be more sceptical. What about you? Where do you think the world is going?

Things are getting worse

Things are getting better

Things go round in a circle of life

Things are in chaos

▷ WATCH: Hope Part 2

- Life is full of many good things. But the Bible is realistic about the darkness we experience too.

- Isaiah 9 speaks to "people walking in darkness". It was a message from God, promising his people a "Wonderful Counsellor, Mighty God, Everlasting Father, Prince of Peace", who would bring light to the darkness (Isaiah 9:6).

- Most of us hope that there's a God out there. The Bible says that there *is*, and that he's come to earth in the person of Jesus. Jesus is the person Isaiah spoke of.

- Jesus calmed a storm on Lake Galilee.

- Jesus raised a dead girl.

- There's only one category big enough for him: Mighty God.

- Jesus proves there is a Mighty God who cares for his world and wants to help people.

- Jesus' miracles point to the end of the story: one day he will bring in full a new world without uncertainty, sickness or grief.

- This is the Christian hope: a joyful expectation for the future, based on true events in the past, that changes everything about the present.

*² The people walking in darkness
have seen a great light;
on those living in the land of deep darkness
a light has dawned ...
⁶ For to us a child is born,
to us a son is given,
and the government will be on his shoulders.
And he will be called
Wonderful Counsellor, Mighty God,
Everlasting Father, Prince of Peace.*

Isaiah 9:2, 6

📖 EXPLORE

1. What most surprised or intrigued you about the Christian view of hope that we've just heard described?

Christian hope claims to be "a joyful expectation for the future, based on true events in the past". The question is: how do we know those events are true? In the film, we heard about one day in Jesus' life, as told by a man named Luke in his "Gospel". So, can we trust Luke's account?

Right at the beginning of his book, Luke describes how he went about compiling his Gospel.

Read Luke 1:1-4

("Luke 1:1-4" refers to Luke, chapter 1, verses 1-4.)

Fulfilled | Brought about; completed.
Eye witnesses | Those who saw first-hand what Jesus said and did.
The word | God's message about Jesus.

Theophilus | A Greek name meaning "friend of God". This was the first, though not the only reader of Luke's book.

---

2. According to Luke, why did he write his Gospel?
   (See Luke 1:4.)

3. How did Luke research the events he wrote about?
   (See Luke 1:2-3.)

4. How does Luke's method help us to have confidence in what
   he wrote about Jesus?

So, the claim is that we're reading the words of a historian who
had carefully researched the events of Jesus' life by speaking
with eye witnesses – including the two events described in the
film. Let's take another look at the second of those events.

Read Luke 8:40-42, 49-56

5. Trace the events of this passage. How might Jairus have felt
   at each of these points?

   • Verse 49

   • Verse 50

   • Verses 51-53

   • Verse 54-55

   • Verse 56

Synagogue | Where Jewish
people gather for worship.

---

6. What does this episode show us about:

• Jesus' power?

• Jesus' character?

7. Earlier, we heard these events in Luke's Gospel described as "a thumbnail preview of an entirely new world" that Jesus will bring about one day. What hopeless situations do you see around you? What difference would it make to how we think and feel about those situations if Jesus were the Mighty God, who would one day step in to set everything right?

8. We've been thinking in this session about how the Bible claims that Jesus is the Mighty God, who gives us a hope worth having. What has particularly struck you as you've watched the films and looked at this part of Luke's Gospel?

SESSION 2
PEACE

▷ WATCH: Peace Part 1

- We're all hoping for peace…
    - "out there"
    - "in here"
    - "between us"

- *Shalom* is the Bible's word for real peace – wholeness, harmony, completeness, prosperity, welfare, tranquillity, safety.

- But is lasting peace only a pipe dream?

⊜ DISCUSS

We've heard about some different ways in which we might be hoping for peace. But what about you? How do you think we can find peace?

**Searching inside
yourself**

**Getting away from
it all**

**Co-operating with
others**

**Campaigning for
change**

▷ WATCH: Peace Part 2

- We all want peace; but the problem is that we all want peace on our terms. We say, "My life, my rules".

- The problem is not just "horizontal". We lack peace on a "vertical" level, between ourselves and our Creator. Instead of saying, "Your world, your rules", we say, "My life, my rules". The Bible calls this sin.

- This matters because God is a God of justice, so God judges sin.

- But there is hope: a Prince of Peace – Jesus.

- Jesus was arrested, put on trial and sentenced to execution by crucifixion. As he was dying, he told the criminal next to him, "Today you will be with me in paradise" (Luke 23:43). Jesus offered him a place of peace beyond death.

- How is this possible? Three steps to paradise: the criminal…
  1) acknowledges his wrongdoing,
  2) recognizes Jesus as the King, and
  3) cries out to Jesus for rescue.

- On the cross, Jesus absorbed God's anger at sin. This is how he can offer us peace.

- If we take Jesus up on his offer, we can start enjoying peace "in here", "between us" and, one day, "out there" too.

📖 EXPLORE

1. Where do you think our problem with peace comes from (if you think we have a problem at all)?

Luke wants to show us that our problem is not just horizontal but vertical – and that as Jesus died, he was dealing with that lack of peace between us and God.

Read Luke 23:32-47

Luke records two supernatural events that happened while Jesus was on the cross. These were signs from God that pointed to what was happening vertically as Jesus died.

2. What was the first supernatural event, recorded in verses 44-45a? What does that suggest was happening vertically as Jesus died on the cross? (See note opposite for more information.)

Casting lots | A way of making decisions randomly (similar to flipping a coin).

Messiah | A Greek word meaning "anointed one"; the King God had promised would rescue his people.

Centuries before, God had spoken through one of his prophets, named Amos. God announced how people could know that his judgment on humanity's sin and on their conflict with him had come: "'In that day,' declares the Sovereign LORD, 'I will make the sun go down at noon and darken the earth in broad daylight'" (Amos 8:9).

God had also told his people to build a "temple" in Jerusalem – a building where he would dwell among them. But, as part of the temple, he had instructed them to put up a huge curtain at least 30 feet (9m) wide and 30 feet high. This curtain functioned as a "KEEP OUT" sign – the perfect God was present on one side of the curtain, and imperfect people could not pass through the curtain to be with him.

3. Look at what happened to the curtain in the second half of verse 45. What does this second supernatural event suggest Jesus' death had achieved?

4. Jesus speaks three times in this passage. What does each tell us about him?

   • Verse 34

• Verse 43

• Verse 46

5. In what ways did the various people around the three crosses respond to Jesus?

• "The people" (verse 35)

• "The rulers" (verse 35)

• "The soldiers" (verses 36-37)

- "The centurion" (verse 47)

6. Which of those reactions best represents the way you're responding to Jesus at the moment?

7. On the night Jesus was arrested, his disciples had let him down, denied him and deserted him. Yet after Jesus had risen from death (which we'll be thinking about more in the next session), he greeted them with the words "Peace be with you" (24:36).

- How did Jesus make peace possible by dying on the cross?

- How do you think it felt for the disciples to hear that greeting? What would it take for you to receive that same peace from Jesus today?

8. We've been thinking in this session about how the Bible claims that Jesus is the Prince of Peace, who came to fulfil our hope of peace. What has particularly struck you as you've watched the films and looked at this part of Luke's Gospel?

SESSION 3
PURPOSE

▷ **WATCH: Purpose Part 1**

- We all want our lives to mean something. We all need purpose. But the reality of death makes us wonder, "What's the point?"

- In our 21st-century Western culture, we tend to deal with the problem of death in one of three ways:
    - We deny it.
    - We downplay it.
    - We despair about it.

- To find meaning in life, we need an answer to death.

💬 **DISCUSS**

We've heard about some different attitudes towards purpose in life. But what about you? Where do you look for a sense of purpose?

Building a successful career

Pursuing happiness

Raising a family

Leaving a legacy

▷ WATCH: Purpose Part 2

- Jesus died on Friday. On Sunday morning, something happened that can rob death of its power and give life the purpose we long for.

- When the women arrived at Jesus' tomb, it was empty. Two angels told them, "He is not here, he has risen" (Luke 24:6).

- This is hard to believe – then as now. The disciples dismissed it as "nonsense", but in the years that followed they gave their lives for this claim. So what changed?

- Later on Sunday evening, Jesus appeared to his disciples and proved that it was really him, really risen.

- Is there a better explanation for the empty tomb and for the transformation in Jesus' followers? The Bible doesn't ask you to shut your eyes and make a leap of faith. Instead, it encourages you to open your eyes, look at the evidence and make a step of faith.

- If the resurrection is true, then it is wonderful. It means that Jesus can be our "Everlasting Father", who sorts out death and gives us meaningful work with an eternal impact. "Always give yourselves fully to the work of the Lord, because you know that your labour in the Lord is not in vain" (1 Corinthians 15:58).

- Will you take Jesus to be your "Wonderful Counsellor"?

EXPLORE

1. Think back over what we've just heard. What most surprised, intrigued or puzzled you about the Christian hope of life beyond death, and how that gives life now purpose?

Throughout this series, we've been thinking about hope as a joyful expectation for the future, based on true events in the past, which changes everything about my present. But can we be confident that Jesus' resurrection is true – that he really did rise from the dead? That's what we'll consider now.

2. Read through the account opposite of that Sunday morning and evening. Underline places where we're being offered evidence for the claim that "[Jesus] has risen!" (verse 6).

Spices | Used in that culture to prepare a body for burial.
The Eleven | Jesus' closest followers.
Strips of linen | What a body was wrapped in before burial.
Broiled | Cooked over a fire.

The Law of Moses, the Prophets and the Psalms | The Jewish Scriptures, written hundreds of years before. These can be found in the Old Testament section of the Christian Bible.

---

¹ On the first day of the week, very early in the morning, the women took the spices they had prepared and went to the tomb. ² They found the stone rolled away from the tomb, ³ but when they entered, they did not find the body of the Lord Jesus. ⁴ While they were wondering about this, suddenly two men in clothes that gleamed like lightning stood beside them. ⁵ In their fright the women bowed down with their faces to the ground, but the men said to them, 'Why do you look for the living among the dead? ⁶ He is not here; he has risen! ...'

⁹ When they came back from the tomb, they told all these things to the Eleven and to all the others. ¹⁰ It was Mary Magdalene, Joanna, Mary the mother of James, and the others with them who told this to the apostles. ¹¹ But they did not believe the women, because their words seemed to them like nonsense. ¹² Peter, however, got up and ran to the tomb. Bending over, he saw the strips of linen lying by themselves, and he went away, wondering to himself what had happened.

[Later that evening]

³⁶ While they were still talking about this, Jesus himself stood among them and said to them, 'Peace be with you.'

³⁷ They were startled and frightened, thinking they saw a ghost. ³⁸ He said to them, 'Why are you troubled, and why do doubts rise in your minds? ³⁹ Look at my hands and my feet. It is I myself! Touch me and see; a ghost does not have flesh and bones, as you see I have.'

⁴⁰ When he had said this, he showed them his hands and feet. ⁴¹ And while they still did not believe it because of joy and amazement, he asked them, 'Do you have anything here to eat?' ⁴² They gave him a piece of broiled fish, ⁴³ and he took it and ate it in their presence.

⁴⁴ He said to them, 'This is what I told you while I was still with you: everything must be fulfilled that is written about me in the Law of Moses, the Prophets and the Psalms.'

Luke 24:1-6a, 9-12, 36-44

3. Which evidence do you find most striking? Are there any claims which you are less convinced by?

4. We've heard that Jesus is the "Everlasting Father", who sorts out the problem of death and gives meaning to life. If Jesus did rise from the dead, what difference do you think it could make to:

• the way we view our own lives? (See 1 Corinthians 15:58.)

• the way we face the reality of death?

5. A Christian is someone who has committed to living with Jesus as their "Wonderful Counsellor" – the one who takes direction of their life. Who else might we be looking to for our direction in life?

• Thinking about all we've seen of Jesus in these three sessions, how do you feel about the idea of Jesus taking direction of your life?

Over the course of *Hope Explored*, we've been thinking about Christian hope as a joyful expectation for the future, based on true events in the past, which changes everything about my present.

6. Looking back over the last three sessions, what have you found most thought-provoking, reassuring or surprising about the Christian view of:

   • the future – where the world is heading and what Jesus promises for the future?

   • the past – who Jesus is and what he did during his time on earth?

   • the present – what difference Jesus can make to our lives today?

CAN WE RELY ON
LUKE'S GOSPEL?

Who? When? Why?

Luke was the author of two books in the New Testament: the Gospel of Luke, which describes Jesus' life, death and resurrection, and a "sequel", Acts, which details the spread of Christianity in the following decades. Luke was a doctor who appears to have become a Christian from a Gentile (non-Jewish) background (Colossians 4:10-14). He was a travelling companion of the apostle Paul on several of his missionary journeys around Europe (see Acts 16:10-17).

Luke was not himself an eye witness of Jesus, but that does not mean his Gospel is unreliable. In the book's introduction, he describes how he "carefully investigated everything from the beginning" and set out to write an "orderly account" of the message "handed down to us by those who … were eye witnesses" (Luke 1:1-3). He did this so that people who had become Christians – including his patron, Theophilus – could "know the certainty of the things you have been taught" (Luke 1:4).

Jesus died, rose again and returned to heaven around AD 30. Luke wrote about 30-50 years later – well within the lifetime of those who lived through the events he recorded, many of whom he lists by name. So Luke had to write accurately. Any inconsistencies between what people had seen and what he wrote would have discredited him.

Has Luke's book changed over time?

How different is Luke's original book from the book that we have today? We don't have Luke's original to compare with the book we call Luke's Gospel. This is normal for ancient documents, since the original copy would have been written on material such as papyrus or parchment, which would have eventually rotted away.

For this reason historians assess the reliability of copies of an original by asking the following questions:

- How old are the copies?
- How much time has elapsed between the writing of the original document and the production of the copies that now exist?
- How many copies have been found?

The table below answers these questions for three widely-trusted historical works and compares them with the New Testament. So we can have great confidence that what we read is what Luke wrote.

For more detail, *Can I Really Trust the Bible?* by Barry Cooper or *Can We Trust the Gospels?* by Peter J. Williams would be good places to start.

	Date of original document	Date of oldest surviving copy	Approximate time between original and oldest surviving copy	Number of ancient copies in existence today
THUCYDIDES' HISTORY OF THE PELOPONNESIAN WAR	c. 431–400 BC	AD 900 plus a few late 1st-century fragments	1,300 years	73
CAESAR'S GALLIC WAR	c. 58–50 BC	AD 825	875 years	10
TACITUS' HISTORIES AND ANNALS	c. AD 98–108	c. AD 850	750 years	2
THE WHOLE NEW TESTAMENT, INCLUDING LUKE'S GOSPEL	AD 40–100	AD 350	310 years	14,000 (approx. 5,000 Greek; 8,000 Latin; 1,000 in other languages)

HOW TO
KEEP EXPLORING

If you have enjoyed *Hope Explored*, why not try a longer course where you can explore the Christian faith in more depth?

- *Christianity Explored* is an informal and relaxed seven-week course. It is focused on Mark's Gospel, one of the accounts of Jesus' life in the Bible. It addresses three big questions: Who is Jesus? Why did he come? And what does it mean to follow him?

- *Life Explored* is a journey through the story of the Bible. Featuring a combination of short films and Bible interaction, it addresses some of the most important questions we can ask: What is the purpose of life? Is there real hope for humanity?

Ask about following your *Hope Explored* course with one of these, or visit **www.hope.explo.red** for more information and resources.

www.hope.explo.red